Small Paper Swan

Sam Sheldon

BookLeaf
Publishing

India | USA | UK

Presentation by *BookLeaf Publishing*

Web: www.bookleafpub.com

E-mail: info@bookleafpub.com

ISBN: 9789358314557

First edition 2023

Night Bird

i watch her fall asleep
and take a deep sigh of relief,
she is safe now,

gone is the repetitiveness,
gone are the racing thoughts,
the words unspoken,

she spreads her wings
and becomes the wind,
enveloped in the darkness,
she flies towards the moon,
the only being that has ever truly seen her
only the two of them know her,
her scars and her soul,

she howls and she laughs
-and she screams,
one with the wind,
loud with the wind,
she is free here,
until her eyes open again,

in the morning
she will be silent once more,

but tonight she keeps dancing with the moon,
Goddess of the dark,
beautiful night bird

Black Cats

don't tell me about black cats,
like the sunflowers don't curl around my arms,
-holding me,
begging me to stay with them

like the wind doesn't whisper my name,
calling me to the wild,

like the moon doesn't return my soul to me
every lunar phase

my mothers sing to me in tall trees,
their messages relayed in fallen leaves

i know of suffering,
i know of injustices,
i know about black cats

Navy Breeze

sometimes in the deepest night,
she comes back to me,
a navy breeze,

she rushes through my hair
and circles my body,
i sense she misses me,
and i her

and though she wants me to return,
with her comes the darkness,
the dizziness,
and the sickness,

she dries my silent tears
that wish for something like her,
and before she convinces me otherwise,
i take in my navy breeze,
and this time
only her

Red Ribbons

5

she reminds me of a time

when i used to wear red ribbons,
around my wrists and ankles,

long ribbons that curled and spun
in the wind behind me as i ran,
dancing with me,

i feel them when i close my eyes
when i'm spinning
until i'm so dizzy
and the tall grass envelopes me,

spit me out,
and take my red ribbons

Small Paper Swan

i am folded,
small and fragile,
with my secrets
stored in the middle,
but you cannot see them,
because i am a paper swan,

poised and precise,
tucked away at my most vulnerable words,
no one will ever know
that i have terrible things—

they touch my wings
and my face,
tender from the wounds
that lie underneath,
they do not unfold me,
but i do not mind,
i do not grow angry from their unknowing,
because they see me as i intend them to

Under The Harvest Moon

i enter the night freely,
skin lit up by the moon,
ready to take me,
through the woods like a wolf,
to crystal lakes,
dark and mysterious,
but also inviting,
as she reflects my guiding light,
as well as my mothers,
the tall and beautiful trees,
cradling me in their shadows,
promising to keep me safe,
i am free here
to be loud
and strong,
dancing with the spirits of my ancestors,
enchantresses who were pulled to the same
moon,
they were as i am,
a priestess of the night

Ivan

8

we don't mourn the snow
that melts into the earth,
now he is like the snow,
beautiful and fragile
and gone the next day—

next season he will come back,
as the suns rays
or an autumn breeze

each season i will look for him

Creature

9

now that my cracks have been revealed
allow me to show you what lies underneath,
peel me back,
and bask in the aroma,
the intoxicating stench of a beast,
-of a banshee
that only brings you back,
because of the addicting curiosity,
the rush of a near death experience,
the venom that leaves my lips,
i am poison
in the shape of a woman

Hysteria

an energy is trying to escape me
through my trembling hands
and voice,
but my vision stops it
with black spots,
and my fingers
with scratches on my skin,
shouting leaves my mouth
in the form of someone else's words—
i hold on tight
with clenched fists
and white knuckles,
my entire vessel holding its breath,
until the exhaustion
forces the energy back in
to be used another day

Lucid Dreaming

today there are no distractions
from the doubting voices,
they sit heavy on my chest,
threatening to take my breath from me,
i risk a few tears,
but i don't dare speak a word,
instead i stay stuck
in a lucid dream-like state,
paralyzed by the hands
that hang over my mouth
and throat,
long fingernails grazing my skin,
testing me—
hoping I'll break
and let out a scream,
or even just a gasp,
so it can reach down
and get its pleasure
taking what is left of me

Home

take me to India,
take me to Australia,
take me to the backyard
by the hand,
wrap me in your arms
and the grass
and the night sky,
seal the hole in my chest,
where the cold wind blows,
show me bright lights
and deep waters,
take me someplace
i've never been before

take me home

Deep Breath

when does the chaos become peace?
i pull lilacs and mountain air
in through my nose
and plant them in my lungs,

when i panic,
it becomes a beautiful hurricane,
spinning with my thoughts—

when i come back,
i am a garden

Revenge

14

you will read my words,
and your eyes will burn,
as well as your fingertips,
i'm letting you down gently
with only an itch
in the back of your mind,
and when you want to relax,
when you want to wind down,
you'll hear my voice
and remember my face,
you'll try to claw me away,
but i'll always remain
as your itch
as your scars

Witching Hour

it's that time of night
when the peculiar come out
and the mysterious calls to you,
they want you to join,
but you know once you do,
you won't see rest again until tomorrow,
because tonight needs you,
you know this,
or else your mind wouldn't be chasing it,
craving it,
hurting for it,
you've been searching all along
for a place of your own,
you didn't know it was the night,
the whispers,
the beautiful and poetic,
stop denying her
and wake up

Margaret

she is safe in unconsciousness,
her secrets tucked beneath sheets
and weight down by blankets,
locked, air tight
until the morning light unseals them
with screams,
her intelligence is a curse,
creating versions of herself
she believes are real,
unknowingly and subconsciously
hanging up mirrors
that make her beauty invisible,
rearranging letters
that read that she's weak,
she is her only enemy,
the poison she has surrounded herself with
is inhaled deep in her lungs
and exhaled is all she has left

Pumpkin Head

the sound of their voices
pierces my skin,
if i cut off my hair
and my ears
with a razor,
maybe the panic
will drown out the sound
of the nagging,
unbearable,
overwhelming
noises—
if i swallow a flame
or pick apart my skin
into little
       tiny
           pieces,
if i create enough of a mess,
maybe they'll take me away from here

Edith

18

i was proud of the control,
my body became a weapon,
sharp and fierce,
but a sword can only be sharpened
so many times,
before it becomes
thin and fragile
and it breaks

Longing

i try to think of moments when i am free from
this,
all of this,
split seconds of time
when a gust of wind blows through me
and around me,
holding me
just for a moment,
or the pull of the earth
at the base of my feet,
grounding me
begging me to open my eyes
to see and feel her,

as much as i crave these times,
i cannot seem to find a way to grasp them,
hold them,
be held by them—
i cannot seem to find a reason why i deserve
them

London

i used to see shadows of a person
and hear voices,
whispers,
i believe her to be a woman,
i call her London,
London of course has no face,
as she is only a shadow,
though in my current state,
i think maybe i can convince myself
that she's some sort of demon
with fangs and black eyes

i have a voice that fights me,
when i want to be better,
or healthy,
or proud,
when i ask for help,
i begin with positivity,
but then my words end negatively
and exhausted,
as if i never wanted to better myself,
i'm incapable of having an uninterrupted
thought,
the voice fights me even through these words,
perhaps it wants to stay secret,

i think maybe this voice is London,
clawing behind my eyes
and tightening my chest
when i try to speak,
making my word contradict themselves,

i want this voice to be London,
because if it's not,
then it's just me—
it's me screaming over my own pleas for help,
and me scratching the hot tears from my eyes,
it's me holding my own self down
with all the strength i have
with a hand over my mouth

and this is scarier than any demon
with fangs and black eyes

Hush

22

the voice of a ghost whispers my name,
it bangs on my door in the middle of the night,
its shadow catches my eye
and its stench lingers
long after it decides I'm unworthy of its games,
i wonder what's worse?
its presence,
or the worry of its return

Stargazer

i'm sorry to the girl
who did her best to get to this point
just for me to cut her down,
to accuse her words of leaving her mouth
broken,
to the woman
who did her best to cope,
to survive,
just for me to wish her voice would come out as
someone else's,
someone who is wiser
and makes more sense,
denying her uniqueness,
i wish i could cradle her,
and soothe her
and tell her she is beautifully,
individually her
and she did perfect
as the amazing,
wild and
capable her